Praise for *My Broken Language*:

"Probing, intelligent, and earnest . . . V
inal play and not a regurgitated version of her memoir is the
implication that an autobiography is common property, not a
house behind a fence. Others' real lives, their true personali-
ties—call them spirits—shiver through us, leaving their mark.
The arts we attend to—literary, religious, choreographic, con-
versational—are what, in the end, make us who we are and set
us on our way."

—Vinson Cunningham, *New Yorker*

"While Hudes's writing—primarily in English, with passages
in Spanish, Spanglish, and Yoruba—is eloquent, poetic, and
detailed . . . The interspersed nonverbal pieces of music and
movement bring elements of abstraction that form a language of their own, exploring the thoughts and images that
defy description by words alone. Together they bespeak the
playwright's titular 'broken language' and her emphasis on
the heightened presence and diverse aspects of the female
body (not material possessions or money) that were a major
part of her legacy."

—Deb Miller, *DC Theater Arts*

"*My Broken Language* is more than just a play: it's a personal
and theatrical archive."

—James Wilson, *Talkin' Broadway*

"Life is art and art is life in Quiara Alegría Hudes's *My Broken Language* . . . Inside the white, affluent space of playwriting, Hudes establishes herself as a conduit of the unpolished
beauty that vigorously molded her. It's a beauty that rarely
has a suitable translator to document, let alone disseminate it,
and she takes on this job as if it were a sacred duty."

—Hayley Levitt, *TheaterMania*

"An irresistible stage piece . . . The triumph Hudes achieves in *My Broken Language* is two-fold. She makes it utterly clear that her primary goal is to let Puerto Rican women know she has seen them, is one of them, and is planting their more-often-than-not untold stories front and center for them to watch themselves as appreciated for who and what they are. She also brings the stories to a larger audience who may have only the vaguest recognition of these women . . . Hudes is establishing herself as one of the foremost playwrights increasingly breaking barriers—and diverse barrios."

—David Finkle, *New York Stage Review*

"*My Broken Language* is a living museum to the Pulitzer-winning playwright's family, constantly in motion, as the perfect cocktail of expression. More than words, visuals and movement are just as necessary to honor her family as English and Spanish are. Every language on its own is broken, insufficient. But together, in *My Broken Language*, they make a complete, sublime whole that celebrates a family's life and legacy."

—Gillian Russo, *New York Theatre Guide*

"*My Broken Language* is heartfelt, and the playwright's triumph in having this story to tell is hard-won. I felt the love and the strength and the loss among the Perez family and found the intimate ambition of the piece both touching and essential."

—Loren Noveck, *Exeunt*

"Engrossing and entertaining, *My Broken Language* is a skillful stage adaptation which sculpts the source material into an entirely new entity as memorable scenes from a life."

—Victor Gluck, *Theater Scene*

My
BROKEN
LANGUAGE

A Theater Jawn

My

BROKEN
LANGUAGE

A Theater Jawn

A PLAY BASED ON THE AUTHOR'S MEMOIR

Quiara Alegría Hudes

THEATRE COMMUNICATIONS GROUP
NEW YORK
2024

My Broken Language: A Theater Jawn is based on the memoir *My Broken Language* by Quiara Alegría Hudes (One World, New York: 2021).

The publication of *My Broken Language: A Theater Jawn* by Quiara Alegría Hudes, through TCG Books, is made possible with support by Mellon Foundation.

TCG books are exclusively distributed to the book trade by Consortium Book Sales and Distribution.

Library of Congress Control Numbers:
2024005577 (print) / 2024005578 (ebook)
ISBN 978-1-63670-198-1 (paperback) / ISBN 978-1-63670-199-8 (ebook)

A catalog record for this book is available from the Library of Congress.

Book design and composition by Lisa Govan
Cover design by Rodrigo Corral Studio
Cover photography by Monika Kozub

First Edition, May 2024

My
BROKEN
LANGUAGE

A Theater Jawn

My Broken Language had its world premiere at Signature Theatre Company (Paige Evans, Artistic Director; Timothy J. McClimon, Executive Director) in New York on November 6, 2022. It was directed by the author. The set design was by Arnulfo Maldonado, the costume design was by Dede Ayite, the lighting design was by Jen Schriever, the sound design was by Leah Gelpe, and the original music was by Ariacne Trujillo Durand; the choreography was by Ebony Williams and the production stage manager was Kaitlin Leigh Marsh. The ensemble was: Zabryna Guevara, Yani Marin, Samora la Perdida, Daphne Rubin-Vega, and Marilyn Torres.

Characters

An ensemble of five actrxs all play a grrrl and the adult Author she becomes, alternating from scene to scene. No need for them to act, speak, or move like one cohesive character. The point is a multiplicity of voices, bodies, and vibez.

They also slide in and out of scenes as cousins, a sister, a mother, and other folx.

These are Philly Rican roles for Latina actrxs. As to age, body size, skin color, accents . . . the more diverse the ensemble, the better a reflection of the actual Perez women.

Pianist

In the premiere, a sixth performer, a pianist, was also part of this world. The musical component of future productions can be determined by the director.

Touch and Body

Any time there is mention of touching or bodily contact, it's an opportunity for the performers to physically connect. That's the transmission. Word becomes flesh. Bruhealing* through a laying on of hands.

*Bruhealing = bruja + healing

First Movement

A pianist enters and plays an upbeat, joyous merengue.

Grrrls enter dancing, like cousins at a family gathering. They may also write in journals and read/dog-ear/scribble in favorite books. They may also light a candle or bring an espresso to Mom's altar.

But mostly they shake their asses.

Eventually—

GRRRLS: My Broken Language.

North Philly.

1988.

I'm ten years old.

AUTHOR: If you won a shopping spree and loaded your cart full of cousins, that was Abuela's house. They streamed in and out, staying for five minutes or two months or eighteen years. They were from Lehigh Ave, South Jersey, Florida, and Puerto Rico. There was always a new one

I'd never met plus the daily rotation of usual suspects. Cousinhood in my big-ass family was a swim-with-the-sharks wonderland.

When Cuca invited me to Six Flags with the big cousins, I was Cinderella being invited to the ball. These weren't the rug rats of the family, my usual crew. Five to ten years my elder, my big cousins were gods on Mount Olympus, meriting study, mythology, even fear.

(As cousins enter—)

CUCA AND AUTHOR: Cuca.

TICO AND AUTHOR: Tico

FLOR AND AUTHOR: Flor.

NUCHI AND AUTHOR: And Nuchi.

CUCA *(Upbeat)*: Proper Catholic wait-until-marriage Cuca.

TICO: Tico, whose eyelashes were freakishly blond for el barrio. Tico, who would babysit Qui Qui and raid her mom's closet, modeling gowns, skirt suits, leotards. The clothes were always put away before the grown-ups got home.

FLOR *(Loud)*: Flor, the lone Perez who could pull Qui Qui onto the dance floor. *(To Author)* Come on, baila conmigo! Qui Qui, think of dancing like a joke and shaking your ass is the punchline.

NUCHI *(Husky and tough)*: Nuchi, in white bike shorts, white sports bra, white hoop earrings, rainbow elekes. Las siete potencias—the seven Lukumí Orishas—orbited her neck in a protective oval. Nuchi, whose towering majesty and righteous thighs were a dare. Try not to stare. Try not to gulp. Try not to feel a wee bit violated.

AUTHOR: Cuca, Tico, Flor, and Nuchi. Saying their names filled me with awe. They had babies and tats. I had blackheads and wedgies. They had curves and moves. I had puberty boobs called nipple-itis. They had acrylic tips in neon colors.

I had piano lessons and nubby nails. They spoke Spanish like Greg Louganis dove—twisting, flipping, explosive—and laughed with the magnitude of a mushroom cloud.

Our trip was courtesy of Coca-Cola. That summer they were running a promotion. Collect a bunch of cans, get a half-price ticket to Six Flags in New Jersey. We piled in a double-wide hooptie with four different size tires and zero operational seatbelts, soda cans clattering in the trunk. Though it cost more, we gassed up in Philly cuz there was duct tape where a fuel cap oughta go and full-service Jersey didn't mess with that crap. Every time we hit a bump, I could hear half-melted ice swish in the cooler, as bodega ham and Wonder Bread took a swim.

(They all pile in a car, squeezed in close.)

I got the hump in the back. My thighs stuck to the pleather seat and pressed up against Flor's warm bare legs. Cuca's shoulder pushed sweatily into mine. Zooming north on the turnpike, my cousins blasted La Mega and yelled Spanish lyrics at passing cars. There was a thick parade of trucks thundering along the highway.

FLOR: Yank your fist like this, Qui Qui!

AUTHOR: An eighteen-wheeler pulled up alongside us, rattling the hooptie with its gravity. Flor pinched my thigh.

FLOR: Go 'head, Qui Qui, don't be afraid!

AUTHOR: She had coined the nickname, coronating me Qui Qui when I was still in Pampers. The childish title always sounded best in her mouth. But now all my big cousins chanted:

COUSINS: Qui Qui! Qui Qui! Qui Qui!

AUTHOR: Finally the cab was level with the back window. The driver's eyes flicked in our direction and I seized the moment, leaning into the cushion of Cuca's shoulder so

I was visible to the outside world, balling my right fist and
cranking an invisible airhorn.

FLOR: Okay, Qui Qui!

AUTHOR: Now Tico told scatological jokes that were Egyptian
to me. The X-rated ones she told in Spanish, cuz my
Spanish sucked—first generation, second generation—
but even the English punchlines flew over my head. I was
certain they entailed sex and poop, but neither word was
used, nor any synonyms I knew. Still, I laughed when they
did. Nuchi giggled through her missing teeth and Cuca
cracked up, then slapped Tico's shoulder hard, cuz she
was corrupting her.

FLOR: And Flor had news about the new roller coaster: the
Medusa!

AUTHOR: Six Flags had been running ads all summer long,
but Flor knew some folks who'd actually braved it. They
returned not just with apocryphal tales of steep drops and
breakneck turns, but with actual-factual shitted shorts.

FLOR: I hope y'all brought clean draws!

AUTHOR: Carsickness was common for me, but today was
different. My thigh started to sweat where it touched
Flor's and my guts felt like stew. AC was not one of the
car's few features. By the time we pulled into the Six Flags
lot, I couldn't un-hunch.

FLOR: Look, Qui Qui, it's a long walk to the ticket booth. By the
time you get there, the fresh air will make you feel better.

AUTHOR: But extracting myself from the backseat seemed
Herculean.

NUCHI: Should we take you home?

AUTHOR: It's just carsickness. It wears off eventually.

TICO: Let me give you a piggyback.

AUTHOR: But at ten years old, I was too heavy for that, plus my
body was limp with nausea.

NUCHI: Should we call Titi Virginia? Qui Qui, you want to talk to your mom?

AUTHOR: No, I just want to take a nap. Please go without me.

TICO: Okay!

(The cousins head off.)

AUTHOR: I curled fetal in the back, eyes throbbing shut, my hair wet spaghetti against the hot pleather, the car now my own personal hell as all four doors slammed.

Later, half-lulled from a knockout slumber, I was vaguely aware of my cousins' voices coming through open windows. They were eating sandwiches on the trunk, spreading mayo on slices.

NUCHI: Who needs mustard?

TICO: Flor, pass me an orange soda.

FLOR: Ey yo, these pork rinds be poppin'.

AUTHOR: Apparently, hours had passed. They compared notes on which roller coasters had the shortest lines, which carnival games gave the most tickets.

CUCA: Wake up, Qui Qui, you feeling better? Want to join us?

AUTHOR: I muttered "no" from the depths of hell and they headed off again. Again, I fell into the blackness of sleep.

As we drove home, I whimpered between stomach pangs. A pathetic, woozy chorus. "Sorry I ruined the day." I was sure it was the last invitation they'd extend.

FLOR: No, bendito, Qui Qui, we felt so bad leaving you like that.

AUTHOR: Flor ordered everyone to roll down the windows, fresh air being good for carsickness, and she tapped my head, gently guiding it to her warm shoulder.

(Author rests her head on Flor's shoulder and drifts off.)

During the ride south, they were subdued. Wiped out and whiplashed after all those rides, but also shielding me from the fun I'd missed. They'd recount the adventures another time. Intimidated as I had been earlier by their adult humor, their compassion came at me in surprising unison. They put on La Mega and listened in silence. By exit 5 . . .

(Tico snores, knocked out. Flor uses Author's resting head as a pillow for her own, drifting into a car nap. Then, one by one, the cousins peel away and the car empties.)

I missed the goodbyes as Flor and Nuchi and Tico were deposited onto various North Philly corners. When we rolled up to American Street, it was just me and Cuca. I crawled straight for Abuela's bathroom—I hadn't gone all day. My guts were throbbing, my back hunched and radiating heat. Though I could uncurl myself enough to unbutton my shorts, pulling them to my ankles felt like Armageddon. At which point I saw my panties. Red, brown, and moist.

 (Calling out) Cuca?!
CUCA: ¿Estás enferma, Qui Qui?
AUTHOR *(To Cuca)*: Is this what a period looks like?

 (To us) Suspended at my ankles, my panties made a horrible hammock. She disappeared down the hall and I heard Abuela's bureau drawers open and shut. Cuca returned with clean, fresh parachute panties.

(Parachute panties magically appear. Maybe they fall from above, like a heaven-sent miracle. Maybe Cuca does a little dance with them, for Qui Qui's benefit.)

CUCA *(Improvising a tune)*: Oh my gah! Qui Qui's a woman now! Qui Qui's a woman now!

AUTHOR: She knew the precise shower temperature to ease the abdominal pressure. Clean and refreshed after, I pulled on Abuela's bargain-bin panties, which were fit for a queen. Cuca brought me two Bayers and a cup of room-temperature water. Then skipped across traffic to buy a box of maxi pads. *(To Cuca)* Don't tell the bodega man! *(To us)* The Always were thick as a Bible and rough as a brown paper bag, two features that struck me as the height of sophistication. Every fifteen minutes I changed them with vigor and industry. One drop of blood, time for a new one.

CUCA: You only need to change them every couple hours.

AUTHOR: But won't the blood, like . . . dirty me?

CUCA: Relax, a little blood never hurt anybody!

AUTHOR: For the balance of the evening, North Philly was an oasis. The *Wheel of Fortune* marathon. My tranquil stomach. A strong night breeze making the screen door slam over and over. Was I a big cousin now? Was I finally one of them? Eventually I dozed off as Vanna White paced with a calm regal smile.

(The pianist begins to play—a soulful piece to mark the gravitas of this milestone, a song like Joni Mitchell's "Hejira.")

FLOR: Asterisk. In a matter of years, Flor, with a laugh warm as September sun, would be plucked from sanity and blown to chaos, a dandelion seed on the devil's breeze. "Drugs," Mom would say. "Before that shit came to el barrio," Mom would sigh, "we were just another poor neighborhood trying to make do. But then came the overnight sensation."

TICO: Asterisk. Soon, Tico—Tico the prankster, the party on legs—stopped visiting Abuela's. One day, Tico wasn't there. Next day, same thing. No word, no note, no explanation. When the test said positive, Tico peaced out. She joined a pilgrimage of young people who found, in New York, a place to live shame-free.

NUCHI: Asterisk. A few years after that, addiction would render Nuchi skeletal. She would become a walking dagger. But for now, the spandex was tight and right.

(As the pianist continues her song, a limpieza bath is prepared with flower petals and herbs, and is then poured over one of the grrrls, who steps forward as our next Author.)

Second Movement

GRRRLS: West Philly.

1991.

I'm thirteen years old.

AUTHOR: My mom was crowned Changó. The Orisha of lightning. As a child, she was known to have "the gift." Now she was ascending in the religion, becoming who she was always meant to be. I knew her less and less.

Sometimes I'd get baños y limpiezas from the elders. But most of the time Mom would send me upstairs.

Many ceremonies—in my home—were off-limits. I guess some mysteries were too powerful, too real for fragile Qui Qui.

One night, by the flow of the downstairs conversation, I knew some heavy shit was underway. Batá drums thickened the atmosphere like humidity. I couldn't make out words. Some voices, I recognized. Sedo, my not-quite-stepfather, who Mom had been seeing for years. Padrino

Julio, Mom's mentor in the religion, his familiar cadence was lilting, with his signature trace of giggle.

An unfamiliar male voice held forth, his authority galloping in on quick words and melodic inflection. No one interrupted or spoke over this powerful man. In their silence, I inferred deference and profound respect. I stood at the upstairs landing for a very long time, leaning over, hand to ear. Who was this houseguest? What did his presence signal?

One step at a time, that's how I descended. Telling myself *turn back* with every inch of progress. Thick was my compulsion to see what scared me the most. Toward the bottom I cursed my own curiosity. I sat in protest, hoping to stall my forward motion. But my desire to advance was strong and I descended the steps in a seated position. At last the living room unfolded before me.

(Mom appears, seated, wearing white.)

Three people sat at the table—Sedo, Padrino Julio . . . Mom? There was no strange visitor in sight. Mom was the stranger. She was a man. From her mouth flowed the voice I heard upstairs. A plosive, nasal Spanish with some dialect spliced in. What creole tongue, what pidgin words these were, I hadn't a clue. A twang of the ancient rode the cadence. By the sound, this was a frisky spirit, and wise. Even the bones in Mom's face were changed. Her slender nose widened, her overbite reversed so that her bottom jaw thrust forward. She was squatter now, her usually soft shoulders broad and firm. Se montó el espíritu.

The men sat with her, alert and listening. Padrino Julio fed her rum and asked questions, the answers to which Sedo transcribed in a marble notebook. He filled the pages quickly, his pen resting only when he needed a new page.

Occasionally Padrino Julio sought clarity before the next question. The spelling of some unfamiliar town, perhaps, that he'd check on later. "Can you repeat that person's name, please?" She-not-she answered, then lifted Bacardí to her lips, tipped the jug, and swigged down a third of the nearly full rum. Surely she would vomit or seize. Aside from a beer during spring cleaning, Mom never drank. But she slammed down the bottle and the interview continued apace.

I wanted to scream, "Stop! You're gonna hurt my mom!" To run and wipe sweat from this face that was not hers, to reach down her throat and yank out the spirit.

(Batá drums sound. Mom begins to move, overtaken by a powerful spirit. Sometimes the spirit gets stuck or battles inside her, other times there is a flow and equilibrium between Mom's body and égun—ancestor.

Finally, it's over and Mom grows still.)

Upright for the first time in more than an hour, Mom lost her balance and collapsed in Sedo's arms. She looked at our living room with vague familiarity: that wallpaper, this table, the stereo. Sedo chuckled, "Welcome back, Negra. You can relax now." "Cuidao," Padrino Julio said when she stood, "all that Bacardí will go to your head." He chuckled as Mom saw the half-empty bottle, dazed. Then she walked out back without so much as a stumble. "What happened?" she asked as night air swallowed them. Padrino Julio and Sedo began to answer as I stared at the still life, searching for clues. My life required explication, and I didn't have the language to make it make sense.

There was something familiar, though . . . my cousins' dancing. How propulsive and insistent their hips were, as if conducted by some magnificent force. Those gatherings were secular, this one was spiritual. And yet, a pulse is a pulse is a pulse. A drum is a drum is a drum. Yes, it was true, and here lay the evidence: dance and possession were dialects off the same mother tongue. I spoke neither. English, my best language, had no vocabulary for the possession nor the dance.

And English was what I was made of. Would my words and my world ever align?

God, give me a space where this fits—all of this loss and life. Give me a language to voice the scream so others can hear and understand, and in the understanding I can be made whole. Make me whole. God, help me find the right words for begin and end because right now the death and the dance overlap in ways that make a mess.

And even as I prayed, I had to laugh because what god, precisely, was I praying to?

Third Movement

GRRRLS: North Philly.

    1993.

    I'm fifteen years old.

(A different Author steps forward and we're inside a public-school classroom.)

AUTHOR: Central was a public academic magnet school that drew kids from all zip codes.

    Sophomore year English. *Gulliver's Travels, Their Eyes Were Watching God, Narrative of the Life of Frederick Douglass.* Page after page of direct hit. They jangled me, and none more than *Death of a Salesman.* My jaw clenched at Arthur Miller's picket-fence tableaus. Willy Loman was sure some throne was his birthright; when it eluded him he grew disconnected, disconsolate.

ENGLISH TEACHER: What do you think, Quiara? You wrote this in your reading response: "The roots of the grass lawn are rotting." Say more.

AUTHOR: It just annoys me how Loman thinks he's tragic. Two sons healthy enough to throw the pigskin. A marriage intact. Like, what's so awful?

ENGLISH TEACHER: You tell me. What's his problem?

AUTHOR: Well . . . Loman's a *Brady Bunch* guy, the kind of patriarch smiling in an insurance ad. The billboards and TV shows make him out to be some kingly provider archetype. And I guess he drank the Kool-Aid and then, like, eventually had to face the fact that he's average. So that's his tragedy. Being average. Which I don't find tragic.

ENGLISH TEACHER: Write that down, everyone.

AUTHOR *(To us)*: Shit, I wrote it down, too.

All these literary heroes paraded their woe like it was some main event. Hamlet brooded, Romeo beat his chest, Willy went mad. When facing the shitstorm of life, why didn't they dance like the Perez women?

(The classroom phone rings—that loud obnoxious detonation specific to school phones.)

ENGLISH TEACHER: Room 114. Mrs. Slepian speaking.

AUTHOR: I was to report to the principal's office.

ENGLISH TEACHER: Bring your backpack, dear.

AUTHOR: How strange, these empty hallways. Most kids were in class. The main office was filled with cigar smoke, which haloed around the principal and obscured his bearded face. He suggested I call home.

PRINCIPAL: Do you have a quarter?

(Author doesn't. The principal hands her one.)

AUTHOR: Should I pay you back?

PRINCIPAL: Nah. *(Signaling)* Alright, be on your way.

AUTHOR: Outside the main office were wooden phone booths. My first quarter was returned: no answer at home. I tried Abuela's house, the coin was swallowed, and the call went through. Screams rang out in the background. Mary Lou was dead.

MARY LOU *(With humor)*: Mary Lou, whose dance moves and exposed midriff always looked slinky times ten. Mary Lou with a wooden rosary often hovering above her cleavage— Jesus pointing down at the sin. Mary Lou whose joy was outrageous. A happy that needed no café, that woke up and let loose on the world. Rejoice was her daily rhythm. She liked to proclaim she was moving to Florida "¡porque aquí no vale!" If she hated the neighborhood, she had a cheerful way of showing it

AUTHOR: On the SEPTA platform midmorning, I stood alone by the subway tunnel. It was cavernous and moist as a grotto. Water traced mineral outlines on walls, pooling by the tracks. Moments before, I had wondered at our Perez resilience compared to the Willys and Romeos. Now I catalogued our disappearances.

It was our fourth death in as many years. Not one of them had made it past their forties. Whatever beast, whatever bloodsickness stalked the Perezes . . . this reaper nipping at our heels . . . it was gaining steam. I had no data about the crack and AIDS epidemics, no sociological grasp of healthcare inequities. I had no sense we were living and dying through a discrete dot on the American timeline— the eighties and nineties. What I did have? Some funeral cards with white angels and Spanish names looping below them . . . Time to add another card to the collection.

Now, SEPTA stations passed as I neared the awful, inevitable wailing.

At Abuela's house I sat in the stairwell, beholding the mourner's parade. The Brooklyn cousins arrived, mascara smeared, passing tissues. The screen door slammed in constant announcement: neighbors and family cycling through, having a smoke on the porch. Mary Lou's mom wailed and hollered upstairs. When Ginny arrived with the boys, little Danito took my hand and looked me in the eye. "I'm sorry for your loss, Qui Qui." Only in elementary school, he was already an experienced griever. Kid had fucking grace.

Ritz crackers went untouched, Gouda cheese grew waxy, a pot of café sat cold on the stovetop. The tabletop was crowded with bouquets. Enrobed in cellophane, a field of carnations.

Through it all, Ashley slumped on the sofa. Eight years old. No doubt replaying the scene from earlier that day: She heard a weird scream, ran downstairs, and discovered her mom, Mary Lou, motionless on the kitchen tiles. A cereal box in her hand. Some Cheerios littering the floor.

Years earlier, when I was only five, Mary Lou had selected me as miniature bride. Hers would be the real thing, a church ceremony with handwritten invitations. Mom sewed me a white gown to replicate Mary Lou's. Beneath a thick white ribbon at the waist, the skirt flared out, an explosion of tulle.

The day of the wedding, Mom pooled the gown in a circle on the floor and said, "Step in," before tunneling it up over my body. Slowly I fed each arm through a delicate sleeve. It took her many minutes to button each pearl up the back.

I stood in the corridor of St. Ambrose Church, hiding in a foyer beside Mary Lou. Our dresses matched perfectly. The only difference was her high heels to my flats.

She marked my cheek with a red lipstick kiss, then smiled a crescent of mischief and snapped open her clutch.

MARY LOU *(Hatching a mischievous plan)*: Heh heh heh heh . . .

AUTHOR: In that quiet moment, as she dug through her purse for makeup, I felt wildly alive. I loved how the lid clicked open, how the pink stick emerged like spiral steps. I loved the waxy wetness as Mary Lou patted a bit of color onto my lips. Her touch was Creator, turning me human.

MARY LOU: Hold still. *(Patting lipstick on Author, hands trembling)* Mira mis manos.

(She models how to smack your lips so the color spreads evenly, which Author imitates.)

There! Your mom's gonna kill me!

AUTHOR: Then I walked the aisle. At the altar stood her sweetheart, a tall Boricua with indio skin. He was handsome and confident like Mary Lou, and only slightly less goofy. Afterwards, one big sloppy kiss later, they ran outside to the North Philly curb, church bells a-ruckus, and dove giddily into an honest-to-god limousine. It had the whiff of importance, which I mistook for permanence.

Soon I would return to St. Ambrose Church, dressed in black head to toe. Soon we'd drive the streets of North Philly. Slow going, a wending path, horns honking toward the cemetery.

(Author gets in the car with Mom.)

Mom, what's an aneurysm?

MOM: Is your sister asleep?

AUTHOR *(Calling toward the backseat)*: Gabi? *(To Mom)* Yeah.

MOM: It's a blood clot in the brain.

AUTHOR: What causes it?

MOM: Genetics.

AUTHOR: Was it preventable?

MOM: No. Mary Lou's brain was a ticking clock, and none of us had a clue.

AUTHOR *(To us)*: In Compagnola Funeral Home on North 5th. At Riehs Florist on Girard Avenue. We had accounts there, we bought funerals on credit.

BIG VIC: Big Vic: age at death, twenty-four.

GUILLO: Guillo: age at death, forties.

TICO: Tico: age at death, early twenties.

MARY LOU: Mary Lou: age at death, twenty-seven.

AUTHOR *(To Mom)*: Are we cursed?

MOM: It's worse being the titi. I changed Mary Lou's Pampers, Quiara. You never changed her Pampers. *(Sighs. Then—)* Should we drive to the art museum?

AUTHOR: She U-turned and drove the curving roadway up toward the monumental sand-colored pillars. At the top of the parking lot she rolled to a stop. I knew what to do. I got out and unhooked the chain. Mom lurched forward, I rehooked the chain in the car's wake and got back in. We pulled slowly onto the museum's grand upper plaza. The fountains were off for the night. No pedestrians, no tourists. There beyond us twinkled the City of Brotherly Love. Gabi, my sister, stayed sleeping in the car. Three years old, she'd grow up never knowing Mary Lou's eyes—full of pure electric joy. I saw now the once-in-a-lifetime opportunity Gabi presented me: the chance to foster a self-loving, not-disappearing Perez girl. Gabi would flourish. She must. It was my job to make sure of it. *That's* how I would grieve my cousin.

(The pianist plays a sly, winking, lovely piece to lure us from the melancholy—something like "Drume Negrita" or "Fleurette Africaine." The grrrls set up overhead projectors.)

Fourth Movement

GRRRLS: Center City.

1994.

I am sixteen years old.

(A new Author steps forward.)

AUTHOR: The Philadelphia Museum of Art. Sunday admission was free before noon. And I didn't have to babysit until night.

I sped through the Early American galleries, in austere shades of red and gray. Gold-leaf frames, hand-turned Chippendales, pasty old patriarchs immortalized in oil. Just beyond, at the building's outer reaches, the contemporary wing was a white-walled affair. Familiar works formed a receiving line. The Warhols, ironic and cheeky. I poked my head into the grotto of Cy Twombly's *Iliam* series to see if I had started liking it since last time. Nope. The lithe Brâncuşis curved hello. The blue Frank Stella was a geometric splat. Two or three breaths before the Chuck Close thumbprints. A moment of reverie before Richard Long's *Limestone Circle.*

My destination was the Duchamps. They beckoned like a bare shoulder at the edge of a dream.

(Author flicks on an overhead projector. She slides a transparency sheet onto the glass. It shows Bicycle Wheel *by Marcel Duchamp.)*

There was the wooden stool with the bike wheel— rebellious.

(Next transparency sheet: Nude Descending a Staircase, No. 2.*)*

There was the cubist nude descending a staircase— kinetic.

(For each piece she mentions, a new transparency sheet is slid onto the glass.)

The *Boîte-en-Valise* was a miniature curio box.

There was repurposed junk—a bottle rack, an infamous urinal.

The *Female Fig Leaf* was a bronze square of innuendo.

Duchamp was a Swiss Army knife, an attic of ideas, a flea market of art jokes. Ribald as a bathroom-stall punchline, with the abandon of a master who'd earned every rebellion.

Tucked within the Duchamps, Room 182 was hidden in the back, the farthest gallery from the museum's front entrance. Last stop, folks. Nothing left to see. It had the footprint of a coat closet and, without windows or light bulbs, was unlit. If you stepped inside long enough, your eyes would adjust to see a wooden door at the end. Primitive, hewn of wide-planked hardwood. Two peepholes glowed, beckoning. I pressed my nose to the wood. A sliver of life-size diorama came into view. A pastoral scene, lifelike, of a nude white woman on the ground, legs akimbo. Her hairless labia were asymmetrical, possibly deformed. One visible breast sagged like a small pouch of rice. The other breast, along with her face, was out of view.

(Now she slides the transparency of Étant donnés *onto the glass and the audience sees the piece.)*

I angled and contorted, tiptoeing, pressing one eye then the other, trying to glimpse her face. No luck. This nude woman—whether resting after sex, or death-pale after murder—lay atop a bed of twigs like some X-rated Jesus in the manger. The oil lamp she clutched had a still-lit flame, so whatever had befallen her was recent.

Étant donnés was nostalgic tableau, crime scene, rape fantasy, dime-store kitsch, and postcoital ciggy, all in one half-glimpse. Denying her face was the work's grotesque thesis. Her warped vagina, front and center, was the only identity the artist imbued on her. I stared and raged and fumed and fantasized. It wasn't just the vagina that drew me. What really shocked was that the cunt was all she got. Not a face, name, or story. It was a complete and effective violence, this omission of personhood. I knew Duchamp had staged, with precision, my warring impulse to see and turn away.

(She flicks off the overhead projector.)

That evening, Mom and Sedo were out. Once my baby sis was sound asleep, I stood before the majestic altar Mom had built. Secretly . . . I had sometimes wished Mom would worship a little bit whiter. There was installation art right here in my living room, but the Western canon didn't provide vocab for all that. Coconuts caked in thick powdered eggshell. Oranges oozing honey and cinnamon. Beaded mazos and embroidered paños in each Orisha's specific color, dedicated urns housing each Orisha's secrets. Eleguá's clay dish, holding a few pennies and pinwheel mints.

I noticed the air pressure in the room. Even touched the stuff. I ate a piece of the Ibeyi's candy (it was stale). I lifted the lid from Olokun's blue jar (inside was something dark and moist). I reached into Ogun's tiny cauldron and touched a bone. In English the word was altar but in Spanish the word was throne. El trono.

(Suddenly inspired, Author grabs a journal and pencil.)

El trono! I leafed past a journal entry about grief. Past a handwritten lyric of AIDS crisis questions. Past an Allen Ginsberg–style rebel grrrl poem. Past some Keith Haring–style doodles and some notes on Duchamp. Past a description of Radio Raheem's sneakers in *Do the Right Thing*. And here was a blank page and here was a yellow pencil and here was Mom's altar and here was proof: I had words for everything except myself, except my home. How could I squeeze Mom's numinous world into words that didn't fit? English felt awkward as a stranger's shoes.

One day I would dream of a museum, a library I might fit into. One with space to hold my cousins, my tías, my sister, mi madre. An archive made of us, that held our concepts and reality so that future Perez girls would have no question of our existence or validity. Our innovations and conundrums, our Rashomon narratives could fill volumes, take up half a city block. Future Perez girls would do book reports amid its labyrinthine stacks, tracing our lineages through time and across hemispheres. A place where we'd be more than one ethnic studies shelf, but every shelf, the record itself. And future Perez girls would step into the library of us and take its magnificence for granted. It would seem inevitable, a given, to be surrounded by one's history.

One day I would dream. But that night, a gulf stretched between me and this language. My language.

I decided to practice. Maybe a Chopin nocturne would help. But there was el trono in the same room as my piano.

(Author practices Chopin, but after a few bars she stops, distracted. She starts again but stops, looking at Mom's altar. Author gets up and unrolls una estera—a straw prostration mat—and lays it on the floor before "el trono," the altar throne. Prostrated, she shakes a rattle, then speaks loudly:)

Eleguá! Olodumare! Yemaya! Babalú-Ayé! Changó! Oshun! Obatalá! Ogun! Oyá! Thank you!

(She gets up, rolls the mat back up, refreshed.)

The Orisha now lingered on my fingers, dancing with the nocturne, and I sensed the dawn of a real bilingualism, appropriate and specific to me.

(The pianist now plays the full nocturne, which underscores the entire following scene.)

31

Fifth Movement

A rice ballet, set to Chopin.

In lieu of dialogue, the lines are printed on placards for the audience to read. One line per card. They may also be spoken if it adds to the effect.

Abuela's recipe for rice.

Rinse, removing any stones.

Abuela used handfuls, not measuring cups.

In her hands were 10,000 yesterdays.

Heat some oil.

Add rice and stir, coating each grain.

Add water. Hear that?

Sizzzzzzzzzzzzzzzzzzzle.

Chisssssssssssssssssssssssssssssssporrotear.

Salt, cover and leave it be.

Watch a telenovela.

Study la biblia.

Forget you were cooking rice.

Hurry to lower the flame.

It burned.

Savor the burnt part the most.

(If rice or discarded placards are on the ground, then cleanup becomes the ballet's climax.)

Sixth Movement

GRRRLS: West Philly.

1995.

I'm almost eighteen.

(A new Author steps forward, pulls on cheap plastic gloves that come in hair dye kits. Nuchi sits near the tub.)

AUTHOR: The water ran in the bathtub, fogging up the mirror, so Nuchi and I had to talk loud above the noise. It was unfamiliar, this chemical assault—I had never dyed hair before. Eyes tearing, nostrils dripping. And yet this toxic process was, incongruously, a platform for intimacy. I squirted goop onto Nuchi's scalp and swirled it in with my fingertips.

NUCHI: Don't forget my hairline in the back.

AUTHOR: The nape of her neck was soft. I pressed the gel in. A vulnerable place to massage a woman, at the small boneless trough between skull and neckbone. My fingers swirled there for a long moment.

NUCHI: Don't forget my forehead and temples.

AUTHOR: Through thin rubber gloves, I felt my cousin's skin, its warm elastic tenderness.

(Author squirts goop atop Nuchi's head, massages the dye into her hair. A playful tenderness.)

(To Nuchi) I'm done. What's step three?

NUCHI: The shower cap. *(Pulling one on)* Now we wait for me to be a blond.

AUTHOR: How long? Check the instructions while I rinse off.

(Author washes her hands. Nuchi holds the instructions, fiddles around with the paper.)

NUCHI: Yo. How much time does it say?

AUTHOR *(Still rinsing off)*: You tell me.

NUCHI: I thought you knew, Qui Qui. I can't read.

AUTHOR: Can't what?

NUCHI: Read, girl. I can't read.

AUTHOR: But didn't you graduate high school? *(To us)* Even as it left my lips, the question felt unkind. What right did I have to demand her credentials? And yet, I needed to know the score. This was seriously fucked. It didn't seem possible.

NUCHI: They just pass you. I just stood in the back.

AUTHOR *(Checking the instructions)*: Forty-five minutes. *(To us)* So in my magnet school, commas in e. e. cummings poems were debated. In her zoned school, invisibility was lauded as life skill. My loud-mouthed cousin shrank herself to a crumb and the school rewarded her compliance with the prize of a diploma.

I wanted to break free from my living room, to run screaming through the streets of Philly, past the monumental art museum, past glistening brownstones, past the white-gloved doormen of Rittenhouse Square, all the way to the Free Library of Philadelphia, to hop up the stairs two at a time and into the stacks and ask James Baldwin or Pablo Neruda: "My cousin can't read and I can. What do I do?" Except that now, praying in the temple of my literary saints was revealed as its own sick privilege.

NUCHI: Nuchi kneeled at the bathtub and bent over its edge, her wet hair like tentacles on the tub floor.

AUTHOR: When was the last time I saw her dance? Wow. Years had passed since I'd spied her hips in motion. Years of grief had been rent upon her—first a father, then a little brother, then a younger sister. Obituaries Nuchi would never read—she was, instead, her brethren's living flesh-and-blood eulogy.

NUCHI: Did it stain my skin? Cheap dye does that sometimes.

AUTHOR *(Checking the nape and hairline)*: Nope. No stains.

NUCHI: Hey, you gon' knock 'em dead at college. I hope they not conceited and shit.

AUTHOR: See you Thanksgiving.

(To us) Every book, a horizon. A world I had no prior access to. An eye-opening.

Books from Mrs. Slepian's class.

Books from Giovanni's Room, Borders, and the Free Library of Philadelphia.

Books from Mom's favorite botánica.

Books purchased by skipping meals for lunch money and walking home to save SEPTA fare.

Qui Qui became two readers, split down the middle as if by an axe.

AUTHOR 3: There was Real Qui Qui who read the book, same as ever.

AUTHOR 2: And there was What-If Qui Qui, who would never unearth the revelations in its pages. Each book became its presence and absence, its voice and silence.

AUTHOR 3: Who would I be without Ralph Ellison?

AUTHOR 2: Who would I be without *Beloved* on the El, North Philly zooming below?

AUTHOR 4: Who would I be without *The House on Mango Street*?

AUTHOR: Those books were definitive experiences. Their impact on me felt unquantifiable yet real as Abuela's palm cupping dry rice. They were recipes for my life's inner feast.

(The grrrls lay books on the ground like stepping stones, forming a path.)

AUTHOR 3: Books on the southbound 5 to the eastbound 42 on piano lesson Tuesdays.

AUTHOR 2: On the northbound Broad Street Line heading to Central.

AUTHOR 3: Books on 49th and Baltimore during trolley delays.

AUTHOR 4: Or on an Independence Hall bench, in the Saturday morning hush.

AUTHOR 3: José Rivera.

AUTHOR 2: Flannery O'Connor.

AUTHOR 4: *for colored girls who have considered suicide/when the rainbow is enuf.*

AUTHOR 2: *The Norton Anthology of Western Literature.*

AUTHOR: *The Way of the Orisa.*

AUTHOR 4: Shakespeare.

AUTHOR 3: Ginsberg.

AUTHOR: Esmeralda Santiago.

AUTHOR 4: *A Coney Island of the Mind.*

AUTHOR 2: Whan that Aprille with his shoures soote / The droghte of Marche hath perced to the roote.

AUTHOR 3: Curiouser and curiouser.

AUTHOR: Each one a stone on my path, guiding me one step further from Nuchi's reality. And yet as I read with double vision, thinking of her often, each book had the strange effect of binding me to her.

(One by the one the grrrls walk the book path and exit the stage. First Author, then Author 2, then Author 3, then Author 4, then Nuchi, and finally the pianist exits.)

Seventh Movement

But before the grrrls are finished exiting—

GRRRLS: Providence, Rhode Island.
> Brown University Grad School for Playwriting.
> 2004.
> I'm twenty-six years old.

(They leave. The stage is empty. One grrrl didn't quite make it through the door. She is our final Author.)

AUTHOR: Though the Perez women wore clothes when necessary, they were butt naked, half naked, and some-what-exposed a lot, too. Any given day at Abuela's, half the jeans would be unbuttoned cuz, *ay comadre ya tu sabes*: PMS, heatstroke, menopause, and Abuela's exagerada servings kept us trapped in perma-bloat. After an El ride north through the desolate landscape, my matriarchs' bodies were natural wonders. Nuchi's eroded cheekbones were my Grand Canyon. Mom's thigh jiggles my Niagara Falls. The tattoo on Ginny's breast my Aurora Borealis. Facial moles like cacti in the sierra, front-tooth gaps like keyhole nebulae. The cellulite over their asses shone with a brook's babbling glimmer. The sag of each tit—big ones and small—like stalactites of epochal formation. Stalactitties! Upper arms of all shapes, sizes, and textures, like varied river stones. And oh (swoon) the guts! Abundant flabdomens, some inhabited by earthworm-shaped stretchmarks. Brown bellies like Philly's own Half Dome.

The nipples you see in skin flicks, dirty rags, and R movies? Bullshit. Ours were a motley combo platter of puffy, inverted, asymmetrical, enormous, dainty, bumpy, smooth, and protrusive that resembled nothing ever glimpsed in commercial media. Some of us had smaller nipples growing out of our main ones—nipples stacked up like Russian nesting dolls.

I remember Ginny's runner legs: thick firm tree trunks. In sepia eight-by-tens, Mom's teenage thighs rocket down from miniskirts, sturdy, willful things. Some fatness was green-mango firm, other fatness pooled and jiggled. Gravity, that universal law, played out differently from one body to the next. Blubber might protrude horizontally and turn your belly into a shelf where you could prop your cafecito, or ripple and drape down like Victorian curtains.

There was so much pubic hair. You could upholster a fucking mansion. By the time I was grown and saw the hairless pussies that had taken over porn? Poor things looked like E.T. in the plastic lab—overexposed, malnour-ished creatures. Save E.T.! Grow some hair!

One of my Brooklyn cousins had a C-section scar thick as a thumb, bisecting her abdomen from pubes up to navel.

Little dots ran alongside it from the stitchwork, giving the appearance of caterpillar feet. Cellulite spilled out on either side of the taut, shiny scar. She would show off her bifurcated belly, jiggle it, tuck it in her jeans like a shirt. There was no small dose of bragging in her demonstrations. "I can't get liposuctions," she said, smiling, "because the fat will eventually pool around the scar again." The scar thickened with each new child and reopening. "Have you seen how the doctors ruined me?" she'd ask, and even if you said yes, she'd unzip. "Witness me, behold."

Abuela often sat upstairs, naked in the AC, slow-rolling stockings over her varicose veins. In this seated, hunched position her pendulous flat breasts cascaded over her tiered belly, two slinkies heading downstairs. I wanted a pair like that one day.

I had Cuca's flat butt and Mom's water-jug belly, but no real narrative you could read on my curves. That's what made me a girl. The messy book of womanhood's flesh was something to aspire to.

Mom had told me once, as she prepared to receive Changó, that initiates' clothes are torn away so they arrive on their great spiritual path as newborns. It shone light on the fleshy world of Mom's home and Abuela's. I understood with retrospective clarity why Titi Ginny, when teaching four-year-old me how to shampoo my hair, did not coach little me from the side of the shower. No, she undressed and stepped in the water, too. She hoisted me to her naked hip and water poured over our connected bodies. Perez nudity was rebirth of a daily order, both a freedom and a strong protection.

That my little sis Gabi was, by eight, one of the toughest kids in third grade came as no accident. You tryin'a step with some dumb-ass recycled fat joke? Best be prepared to have your buck teeth, onion armpits, or mummy breath flung right back at your donkey face. She threw insults like party snaps, quick blacktop detonations. Most fat jokes, Gabi had learned, are generic low-brain-cell taunts. They hurt, yeah, but not from artfulness. Gabi would spit some bespoke shit your way. Now all of third grade knows you snack on your boogers during science *plus* you're an idiot who can't clap back. Double victory. Yeah, sure, Gabi would be quiet the whole subway ride home. Yeah, sure, she'd disappear into her room without saying hi to Pop. Better to weep into her pillow than talk about it. Cuz if Pop got wind? "Well, then, lose some weight! You're too fat!" I'd pray myself to sleep: *Dear god, let her thrive.* You don't want kids to develop grit that coarse.

Medium grit sure would be nicer.

(Author sits at a writing desk. There's a computer keyboard. Pens and pencils scattered. Loose-leaf sheets and journals.)

The Perez bodies became a play. After a decade-long boycott, "fat" made an energized return. Now I could own the slur, twist its intention, transform it into an honorific. "Queer," "bitch," "dyke," "witch," "slut," and "whore" joined my reclaimed lexicon. In my play they became high praise, a code for belonging.

I wrote the one-act play in my corner apartment. My desk looked out onto the street, just above eye-level with pedestrians. Between classes, students ambled back and forth in cloud drifts. Snippets of conversation bled in. The blue-collar construction workers next door said "Fuck!" from sunup till three P.M. As writing nooks go, none could be more romantic.

Every morning I lit a candle, played batá music, and warmed up by improvising a poem for Oshun, Orisha of female sensuality. All those naked bodies lived in me again, as did the ways I'd been told to despise them.

I brought the pages into playwriting workshop. The feedback was positive. *More,* my colleagues urged. *How could it end there? Give us Act Two!* my teacher said. *Make it full-length and I'll produce it as your thesis.*

How to continue? Act Two eluded me. The desk began to mock. I had run out of ideas and inspiration. The passersby became distractions. The construction workers were now assholes imposing on my peace. The play gained a strong resistance to my efforts.

I needed a Plan B. One night I left for the graduate computer cluster after dinner. White particleboard desks stretched beneath fluorescent lights. No dividers. Just row after row of overworked computers. The cluster was packed.

(She types.)

Around ten, I was plodding along on Act Two. The play was styled as a flesh-and-blood comic book. There were sidekicks, fight scenes, chase sequences, all told through a bi-curious Latina's coming of age. It was raunchy, X-rated. The lead character was a fictional chubby Latina who captured my little sis, Gabi's, essence. I had enjoyed having the Orisha of sweet rivers usher in a girl's first wet dream. But where to next? What sort of ending was I building to?

(A tremor courses through her hand. Then knees. Then shoulders. She tries to still these physical impulses, and is

momentarily successful, but the shaking soon returns in new parts of her body.

The "possession" intensifies. Author is out of her chair, on the floor, moving in a manner beyond her control, transformed. And then suddenly, it's over.)

Time had elapsed: three hours. It was one in the morning. The page count read 87. Last I remembered, there were half as many. On the screen were the words: "End of play."

I scrolled back to page forty and began to read. The comic book vibe quickly morphed into horror. This was not what I had in mind. The play's mounting fury seemed imported from a stranger, but I was that stranger.

In the final scene, the bad guys moved in close, poised to kill my superhero. She made one final declaration on her dying breath.

I AM A WHORE.

Blackout. End of play. *(Confused)* What the . . . ?

I AM A WHORE.

That wasn't the play I wanted to write! I highlighted the text, finger just above the delete key.

Was this what I signed up for? Was speaking the Perez wounds reopening them? Having left myself in those unremembered hours, did I know myself at last?

I am a whore . . .

And I was ten-year-old me again. The year I got my period and sprouted boobs and a man on the corner seized my arm, yanked me so his lips brushed my earlobe, and hot-whispered: *whoooooooore.* "Mom, what's a whore?" How she craned her neck to god and whatever quiet answer she received put a smile on her face. "Una azada," she had declared, describing the ancient tool with a sharp blade for turning the soil. How when the earth gets tired, a hoe breaks the earth, a hoe wounds the earth, digging narrow trenches so you can plant seeds. How we were not whores, we were hoes, plowing our reality, planting seeds of potential. "He thought he was shaming you, Qulara, but he had no clue he was praising you," she had said. "But Mom, how can that be?"

(Appearing in the audience, we see—)

MARY LOU: Mary Lou: years of life, twenty-seven.

BIG VIC: Big Vic: years of life, twenty-four.

GUILLO: Guillo: years of life, forty-something.

TICO: Tico: years of life, twenty and change.

GABI: Gabi: years of life, to be determined.

AUTHOR: I pressed Control-S. save. Lingered in my chair. I printed the play and collected warm pages. The final line, which I was unable to delete, had become a part of the material world, slumping in my backpack above pens and candy wrappers.

I exited into the dark Providence night. Quickstepped home and climbed into bed. The slightest awareness swam through me that night. Was I a big cousin now? Was I finally one of them? Had I, at last, learned to dance?

In a matter of months houselights would dim, ink on paper would become actor's voice on audience ears, and I would tremble, hermana, as you saw the anarchical yarn I had spun from the Perez body.

(Gabi sits beside Author, as though they're seated for a play.)

As you witnessed, at fourteen, a roomful of strangers
witnessing you. But seated at your side in that dark theater, fear convinced me my words were a knife in your
back, my play was a sisterhood-annihilating machine.
Seconds after that final line was spoken, houselights rose,
folks filed to the lobby, and I would admit these fears,
needing to know: *(To Gabi)* Are we through, did I break
us?

GABI: Yeah it hurt . . . but I feel seen. I feel, like, I don't know,
like, fuckin' powerful. I'm a lead character of a whole play,
yo! Thass a honor! Thass right, people, y'all better hear
my story!

AUTHOR: You would tell me, hermana mía, that your grip on
shame had loosened a bit.

Mami,

(Mami sits beside them.)

primas,

(Cuca and Nuchi sit beside them.)

hermana, no one else qualifies for the job. We must be our
own librarians because we alone are literate in our bodies. By naming our pain and voicing our imperfections, we
declare our tremendous survival.

Our archive is in us and of us. The hum of our bodies
together is nothing less than the book of our genius. That
is why, on opening nights, you sit beside me and I touch
you. Your elbow perches on the armrest, my hand finds
the flat smoosh of your knuckles, and we watch our old
silences become loud songs. We are here.

(The pianist reenters and plays as the grrrls touch each other's knuckles atop the armrests, looking out at us.)

END

QUIARA ALEGRÍA HUDES is the Pulitzer Prize–winning play-wright of *Water by the Spoonful*; author of the memoir *My Broken Language*; and screenwriter of *Vivo*. For Broadway, she wrote the book for the Tony Award–winning musical, *In the Heights*, as well as the screenplay for its film adaptation. Her essays have appeared in *The Nation*, *The Cut*, *New York Times*, *Washington Post*, and *American Theatre*. With her cousin, Hudes cofounded Emancipated Stories to help incarcerated people share one page of their life story with the world.